SPORTS AND CLASSIC CAR TRAVEL JOURNAL

Ken McLeod

Speller Press

Beverley England

Sports and Classic Car Travel Journal

Copyright © 2020 Ken McLeod

All Rights Reserved.

No part of this publication may be reproduced, stored in a retrieval system, or transmitted in any form or by any means, electronic, mechanical, photocopy, recording, or otherwise, without the prior permission of the copyright holder Ken McLeod and the below publisher of this book.

Published by Speller Press
ISBN 978-1-9163641-0-3

Speller Press
publish@spellerpress.com
www.spellerpress.com
Publisher Ref: SP-KJM-SCCTJ-2020-V1

www.instagram.com/speller_press
www.pinterest.co.uk/publish3850
www.facebook.com/spellerpress
www.twitter.com/SpellerPress

Sports and Classic Car Travel Journal

Welcome to the Sports and Classic Car Travel Journal, a trusted friend that it will accompany you on many future touring adventures.

The Sports and Classic Car Travel Journal provides you with a valuable instrument in which to chronicle each leg of your motoring journey, charting significant outings and grand tours.

Split into four, seven-day tours; the journal offers plenty of space for recording personal and vehicle information, planning the day, recording data and documenting all treasured meetings and unusual events encountered throughout your journey.

Designed as a keepsake, or as a document to afford provenance to your vehicle, the Sports and Classic Car Travel Journal will only add value to your very precious investment, and serve as a reminder of many happy memories.

Registered Owner Details

Name

Company Name

Contact Address

Contact Telephone
Home:-

Mobile:-

Office:-

Contact Email
Home:-

Office:-

Date Vehicle Purchased

Date Vehicle Sold

Vehicle Details

Vehicle Make

Vehicle Model / Series

Vehicle Body Style / Number

Registration Number

Private Registration Number

Date of Registration

Vehicle Identification Number

Vehicle Details

Engine Capacity

Engine Series / Number

Fuel Category

Vehicle Colour

Additional Information

Grand Tour

1

Grand Tour

Driver

Co-driver

Passengers

1:-

2:-

3:-

Tour Start

Time:-

Date:-

Tour End

Time:-

Date:-

Grand Tour

Tour Start

Location:-

Tour Destination

Location:-

Tour Start Odometer

Reading:-

Tour End Odometer

Reading:-

Total Tour Distance

Kilometres:-

Miles:-

Grand Tour

Total Tour Fuel Consumption

Litres:-

Imperial Gallons:-

US Gallons:-

Tour Fuel

Total Costs:-

Repairs

Total Cost:-

Additional Information

TRAVEL PLANS

Daily Travel Journal

Date

Weather Conditions

Odometer Reading

Start:-

Finish:-

Total Distance Travelled:-

Fuel Level Reading

Start:-

Finish:-

Start Driving Day

Time:-

Location:-

Daily Travel Journal

Route / Roads Toured

Routine Pitstops

Location:-

Fuel Quantity:-

Lubricants:-

Extras:-

Total Cost:-

Rest Stops

Location:-

Finish Driving Day

Time:-

Location:-

ADDITIONAL NOTES

TRAVEL PLANS

Daily Travel Journal

Date

Weather Conditions

Odometer Reading

Start:-

Finish:-

Total Distance Travelled:-

Fuel Level Reading

Start:-

Finish:-

Start Driving Day

Time:-

Location:-

Daily Travel Journal

Route / Roads Toured

Routine Pitstops

Location:-

Fuel Quantity:-

Lubricants:-

Extras:-

Total Cost:-

Rest Stops

Location:-

Finish Driving Day

Time:-

Location:-

ADDITIONAL NOTES

TRAVEL PLANS

Daily Travel Journal

Date

Weather Conditions

Odometer Reading

Start:-

Finish:-

Total Distance Travelled:-

Fuel Level Reading

Start:-

Finish:-

Start Driving Day

Time:-

Location:-

Daily Travel Journal

Route / Roads Toured

Routine Pitstops

Location:-

Fuel Quantity:-

Lubricants:-

Extras:-

Total Cost:-

Rest Stops

Location:-

Finish Driving Day

Time:-

Location:-

ADDITIONAL NOTES

TRAVEL PLANS

Daily Travel Journal

Date

Weather Conditions

Odometer Reading

Start:-

Finish:-

Total Distance Travelled:-

Fuel Level Reading

Start:-

Finish:-

Start Driving Day

Time:-

Location:-

Daily Travel Journal

Route / Roads Toured

Routine Pitstops

Location:-

Fuel Quantity:-

Lubricants:-

Extras:-

Total Cost:-

Rest Stops

Location:-

Finish Driving Day

Time:-

Location:-

ADDITIONAL NOTES

TRAVEL PLANS

Daily Travel Journal

Date

Weather Conditions

Odometer Reading

Start:-

Finish:-

Total Distance Travelled:-

Fuel Level Reading

Start:-

Finish:-

Start Driving Day

Time:-

Location:-

Daily Travel Journal

Route / Roads Toured

Routine Pitstops

Location:-

Fuel Quantity:-

Lubricants:-

Extras:-

Total Cost:-

Rest Stops

Location:-

Finish Driving Day

Time:-

Location:-

ADDITIONAL NOTES

TRAVEL PLANS

Daily Travel Journal

Date

Weather Conditions

Odometer Reading

Start:-

Finish:-

Total Distance Travelled:-

Fuel Level Reading

Start:-

Finish:-

Start Driving Day

Time:-

Location:-

Daily Travel Journal

Route / Roads Toured

Routine Pitstops

Location:-

Fuel Quantity:-

Lubricants:-

Extras:-

Total Cost:-

Rest Stops

Location:-

Finish Driving Day

Time:-

Location:-

ADDITIONAL NOTES

TRAVEL PLANS

Daily Travel Journal

Date

Weather Conditions

Odometer Reading

Start:-

Finish:-

Total Distance Travelled:-

Fuel Level Reading

Start:-

Finish:-

Start Driving Day

Time:-

Location:-

Daily Travel Journal

Route / Roads Toured

Routine Pitstops

Location:-

Fuel Quantity:-

Lubricants:-

Extras:-

Total Cost:-

Rest Stops

Location:-

Finish Driving Day

Time:-

Location:-

ADDITIONAL NOTES

Grand Tour 2

Grand Tour

Driver

Co-driver

Passengers

1:-

2:-

3:-

Tour Start

Time:-

Date:-

Tour End

Time:-

Date:-

Grand Tour

Tour Start

Location:-

Tour Destination

Location:-

Tour Start Odometer

Reading:-

Tour End Odometer

Reading:-

Total Tour Distance

Kilometres:-

Miles:-

Grand Tour

Total Tour Fuel Consumption

Litres:-

Imperial Gallons:-

US Gallons:-

Tour Fuel

Total Costs:-

Repairs

Total Cost:-

Additional Information

Sports and Classic Car Travel Journal

TRAVEL PLANS

Daily Travel Journal

Date

Weather Conditions

Odometer Reading

Start:-

Finish:-

Total Distance Travelled:-

Fuel Level Reading

Start:-

Finish:-

Start Driving Day

Time:-

Location:-

Daily Travel Journal

Route / Roads Toured

Routine Pitstops

Location:-

Fuel Quantity:-

Lubricants:-

Extras:-

Total Cost:-

Rest Stops

Location:-

Finish Driving Day

Time:-

Location:-

ADDITIONAL NOTES

TRAVEL PLANS

Daily Travel Journal

Date

Weather Conditions

Odometer Reading

Start:-

Finish:-

Total Distance Travelled:-

Fuel Level Reading

Start:-

Finish:-

Start Driving Day

Time:-

Location:-

Daily Travel Journal

Route / Roads Toured

Routine Pitstops

Location:-

Fuel Quantity:-

Lubricants:-

Extras:-

Total Cost:-

Rest Stops

Location:-

Finish Driving Day

Time:-

Location:-

ADDITIONAL NOTES

TRAVEL PLANS

Daily Travel Journal

Date

Weather Conditions

Odometer Reading

Start:-

Finish:-

Total Distance Travelled:-

Fuel Level Reading

Start:-

Finish:-

Start Driving Day

Time:-

Location:-

Daily Travel Journal

Route / Roads Toured

Routine Pitstops

Location:-

Fuel Quantity:-

Lubricants:-

Extras:-

Total Cost:-

Rest Stops

Location:-

Finish Driving Day

Time:-

Location:-

ADDITIONAL NOTES

TRAVEL PLANS

Daily Travel Journal

Date

Weather Conditions

Odometer Reading

Start:-

Finish:-

Total Distance Travelled:-

Fuel Level Reading

Start:-

Finish:-

Start Driving Day

Time:-

Location:-

Daily Travel Journal

Route / Roads Toured

Routine Pitstops

Location:-

Fuel Quantity:-

Lubricants:-

Extras:-

Total Cost:-

Rest Stops

Location:-

Finish Driving Day

Time:-

Location:-

ADDITIONAL NOTES

TRAVEL PLANS

Daily Travel Journal

Date

Weather Conditions

Odometer Reading

Start:-

Finish:-

Total Distance Travelled:-

Fuel Level Reading

Start:-

Finish:-

Start Driving Day

Time:-

Location:-

Daily Travel Journal

Route / Roads Toured

Routine Pitstops

Location:-

Fuel Quantity:-

Lubricants:-

Extras:-

Total Cost:-

Rest Stops

Location:-

Finish Driving Day

Time:-

Location:-

ADDITIONAL NOTES

TRAVEL PLANS

Daily Travel Journal

Date

Weather Conditions

Odometer Reading

Start:-

Finish:-

Total Distance Travelled:-

Fuel Level Reading

Start:-

Finish:-

Start Driving Day

Time:-

Location:-

Daily Travel Journal

Route / Roads Toured

Routine Pitstops

Location:-

Fuel Quantity:-

Lubricants:-

Extras:-

Total Cost:-

Rest Stops

Location:-

Finish Driving Day

Time:-

Location:-

ADDITIONAL NOTES

TRAVEL PLANS

Daily Travel Journal

Date

Weather Conditions

Odometer Reading

Start:-

Finish:-

Total Distance Travelled:-

Fuel Level Reading

Start:-

Finish:-

Start Driving Day

Time:-

Location:-

Daily Travel Journal

Route / Roads Toured

Routine Pitstops

Location:-

Fuel Quantity:-

Lubricants:-

Extras:-

Total Cost:-

Rest Stops

Location:-

Finish Driving Day

Time:-

Location:-

ADDITIONAL NOTES

Grand Tour
3

Grand Tour

Driver

Co-driver

Passengers

1:-

2:-

3:-

Tour Start

Time:-

Date:-

Tour End

Time:-

Date:-

Grand Tour

Tour Start

Location:-

Tour Destination

Location:-

Tour Start Odometer

Reading:-

Tour End Odometer

Reading:-

Total Tour Distance

Kilometres:-

Miles:-

Grand Tour

Total Tour Fuel Consumption

Litres:-

Imperial Gallons:-

US Gallons:-

Tour Fuel

Total Costs:-

Repairs

Total Cost:-

Additional Information

TRAVEL PLANS

Daily Travel Journal

Date

Weather Conditions

Odometer Reading

Start:-

Finish:-

Total Distance Travelled:-

Fuel Level Reading

Start:-

Finish:-

Start Driving Day

Time:-

Location:-

Daily Travel Journal

Route / Roads Toured

Routine Pitstops

Location:-

Fuel Quantity:-

Lubricants:-

Extras:-

Total Cost:-

Rest Stops

Location:-

Finish Driving Day

Time:-

Location:-

ADDITIONAL NOTES

TRAVEL PLANS

Daily Travel Journal

Date

Weather Conditions

Odometer Reading

Start:-

Finish:-

Total Distance Travelled:-

Fuel Level Reading

Start:-

Finish:-

Start Driving Day

Time:-

Location:-

Daily Travel Journal

Route / Roads Toured

Routine Pitstops

Location:-

Fuel Quantity:-

Lubricants:-

Extras:-

Total Cost:-

Rest Stops

Location:-

Finish Driving Day

Time:-

Location:-

ADDITIONAL NOTES

TRAVEL PLANS

Daily Travel Journal

Date

Weather Conditions

Odometer Reading

Start:-

Finish:-

Total Distance Travelled:-

Fuel Level Reading

Start:-

Finish:-

Start Driving Day

Time:-

Location:-

Daily Travel Journal

Route / Roads Toured

Routine Pitstops

Location:-

Fuel Quantity:-

Lubricants:-

Extras:-

Total Cost:-

Rest Stops

Location:-

Finish Driving Day

Time:-

Location:-

ADDITIONAL NOTES

TRAVEL PLANS

Daily Travel Journal

Date

Weather Conditions

Odometer Reading

Start:-

Finish:-

Total Distance Travelled:-

Fuel Level Reading

Start:-

Finish:-

Start Driving Day

Time:-

Location:-

Daily Travel Journal

Route / Roads Toured

Routine Pitstops

Location:-

Fuel Quantity:-

Lubricants:-

Extras:-

Total Cost:-

Rest Stops

Location:-

Finish Driving Day

Time:-

Location:-

ADDITIONAL NOTES

TRAVEL PLANS

Daily Travel Journal

Date

Weather Conditions

Odometer Reading

Start:-

Finish:-

Total Distance Travelled:-

Fuel Level Reading

Start:-

Finish:-

Start Driving Day

Time:-

Location:-

Daily Travel Journal

Route / Roads Toured

Routine Pitstops

Location:-

Fuel Quantity:-

Lubricants:-

Extras:-

Total Cost:-

Rest Stops

Location:-

Finish Driving Day

Time:-

Location:-

ADDITIONAL NOTES

TRAVEL PLANS

Daily Travel Journal

Date

Weather Conditions

Odometer Reading

Start:-

Finish:-

Total Distance Travelled:-

Fuel Level Reading

Start:-

Finish:-

Start Driving Day

Time:-

Location:-

Daily Travel Journal

Route / Roads Toured

Routine Pitstops

Location:-

Fuel Quantity:-

Lubricants:-

Extras:-

Total Cost:-

Rest Stops

Location:-

Finish Driving Day

Time:-

Location:-

ADDITIONAL NOTES

Sports and Classic Car Travel Journal

TRAVEL PLANS

Daily Travel Journal

Date

Weather Conditions

Odometer Reading

Start:-

Finish:-

Total Distance Travelled:-

Fuel Level Reading

Start:-

Finish:-

Start Driving Day

Time:-

Location:-

Daily Travel Journal

Route / Roads Toured

Routine Pitstops

Location:-

Fuel Quantity:-

Lubricants:-

Extras:-

Total Cost:-

Rest Stops

Location:-

Finish Driving Day

Time:-

Location:-

ADDITIONAL NOTES

Grand Tour 4

Grand Tour

Driver

Co-driver

Passengers

1:-

2:-

3:-

Tour Start

Time:-

Date:-

Tour End

Time:-

Date:-

Grand Tour

Tour Start

Location:-

Tour Destination

Location:-

Tour Start Odometer

Reading:-

Tour End Odometer

Reading:-

Total Tour Distance

Kilometres:-

Miles:-

Grand Tour

Total Tour Fuel Consumption

Litres:-

Imperial Gallons:-

US Gallons:-

Tour Fuel

Total Costs:-

Repairs

Total Cost:-

Additional Information

TRAVEL PLANS

Daily Travel Journal

Date

Weather Conditions

Odometer Reading

Start:-

Finish:-

Total Distance Travelled:-

Fuel Level Reading

Start:-

Finish:-

Start Driving Day

Time:-

Location:-

Daily Travel Journal

Route / Roads Toured

Routine Pitstops

Location:-

Fuel Quantity:-

Lubricants:-

Extras:-

Total Cost:-

Rest Stops

Location:-

Finish Driving Day

Time:-

Location:-

ADDITIONAL NOTES

TRAVEL PLANS

Daily Travel Journal

Date

Weather Conditions

Odometer Reading

Start:-

Finish:-

Total Distance Travelled:-

Fuel Level Reading

Start:-

Finish:-

Start Driving Day

Time:-

Location:-

Daily Travel Journal

Route / Roads Toured

Routine Pitstops

Location:-

Fuel Quantity:-

Lubricants:-

Extras:-

Total Cost:-

Rest Stops

Location:-

Finish Driving Day

Time:-

Location:-

ADDITIONAL NOTES

TRAVEL PLANS

Daily Travel Journal

Date

Weather Conditions

Odometer Reading

Start:-

Finish:-

Total Distance Travelled:-

Fuel Level Reading

Start:-

Finish:-

Start Driving Day

Time:-

Location:-

Daily Travel Journal

Route / Roads Toured

Routine Pitstops

Location:-

Fuel Quantity:-

Lubricants:-

Extras:-

Total Cost:-

Rest Stops

Location:-

Finish Driving Day

Time:-

Location:-

ADDITIONAL NOTES

TRAVEL PLANS

Daily Travel Journal

Date

Weather Conditions

Odometer Reading

Start:-

Finish:-

Total Distance Travelled:-

Fuel Level Reading

Start:-

Finish:-

Start Driving Day

Time:-

Location:-

Daily Travel Journal

Route / Roads Toured

Routine Pitstops

Location:-

Fuel Quantity:-

Lubricants:-

Extras:-

Total Cost:-

Rest Stops

Location:-

Finish Driving Day

Time:-

Location:-

ADDITIONAL NOTES

TRAVEL PLANS

Daily Travel Journal

Date

Weather Conditions

Odometer Reading

Start:-

Finish:-

Total Distance Travelled:-

Fuel Level Reading

Start:-

Finish:-

Start Driving Day

Time:-

Location:-

Daily Travel Journal

Route / Roads Toured

Routine Pitstops

Location:-

Fuel Quantity:-

Lubricants:-

Extras:-

Total Cost:-

Rest Stops

Location:-

Finish Driving Day

Time:-

Location:-

ADDITIONAL NOTES

TRAVEL PLANS

Daily Travel Journal

Date

Weather Conditions

Odometer Reading

Start:-

Finish:-

Total Distance Travelled:-

Fuel Level Reading

Start:-

Finish:-

Start Driving Day

Time:-

Location:-

Daily Travel Journal

Route / Roads Toured

Routine Pitstops

Location:-

Fuel Quantity:-

Lubricants:-

Extras:-

Total Cost:-

Rest Stops

Location:-

Finish Driving Day

Time:-

Location:-

ADDITIONAL NOTES

TRAVEL PLANS

Daily Travel Journal

Date

Weather Conditions

Odometer Reading

Start:-

Finish:-

Total Distance Travelled:-

Fuel Level Reading

Start:-

Finish:-

Start Driving Day

Time:-

Location:-

Daily Travel Journal

Route / Roads Toured

Routine Pitstops

Location:-

Fuel Quantity:-

Lubricants:-

Extras:-

Total Cost:-

Rest Stops

Location:-

Finish Driving Day

Time:-

Location:-

ADDITIONAL NOTES

www.ingramcontent.com/pod-product-compliance
Lightning Source LLC
Chambersburg PA
CBHW071738080526
44588CB00013B/2074